ICE CREAMS
& SORBETS

Valerie Ferguson

LORENZ BOOKS

Contents

Recipes

Introduction

Everyone loves ice creams and sorbets – they bring a touch of luxury to any occasion. There is still nothing to compare with a home-made ice or sorbet prepared from the finest ingredients. They are quite stunning, and ice cream in particular lends itself to endless variations in flavour and texture.

Ice creams and sorbets are ideal for entertaining as they can be prepared well in advance. They are also surprisingly simple to make. An ice cream maker is not essential (though it makes the task even easier): you can achieve fabulous results without one, using the most basic equipment. Just remember to turn the freezer to its coldest setting about 30 minutes ahead of time. Before serving, transfer the frozen ice cream or sorbet to the refrigerator for 30 minutes to soften.

Whether you wish to capture the freshness of summer fruits such as strawberries and apricots or feast on chocolate and nuts, indulge in a wonderfully rich ice cream dessert or cut the calories with a delicious low-fat ice or sparkling sorbet, you will find a recipe in this book to suit your taste.

Why not treat yourself to a little luxury? Once you have tasted home-made ice creams and sorbets, you will be completely captivated by their satisfying richness.

Techniques

COOKED FRUIT PURÉE

A wide range of fruit purées are a useful base for many ice creams and sorbets, and they also make very good fat-free sauces.

1 Wash the fruit in cold water. Remove the stones and cook the fruit in a pan, with a small amount of water or sugar, until soft. If you are using sugar alone, heat the fruit very gently until the fruit juice begins to run and the sugar dissolves.

2 Tip the cooked fruit into a food processor or blender and process until smooth. The mixture may then need to be sieved (strained).

SIEVING FRUIT

Many recipes call for fruit to be sieved (strained), to remove pips or skin. Firmer fruit, such as apples, should be cooked before you sieve them; soft fruit, like raspberries, can be sieved raw and spooned straight on to the plate.

1 If the fruit is firm, purée it first in a blender or food processor. Tip it into a sieve (strainer) over a large bowl.

2 Using a ladle or wooden spoon, rub the purée firmly through the sieve, until all the soft pulp is in the bowl and just the pips or fibrous matter are left in the sieve.

SEPARATING EGGS

There are many ways to separate eggs, but this simple method is by far the easiest.

1 Tap the egg sharply against the edge of a mixing bowl to break the shell across the middle.

2 Holding the egg over the bowl, carefully pull the two halves of shell apart and gently tip the yolk from one half to the other, allowing the white to run into the bowl.

COOK'S TIP: It is not advisable for pregnant women, the very young or elderly to eat raw eggs.

WHISKING EGG WHITES

Egg whites can increase in volume by about eight times, making mixtures light and airy.

1 Place the egg whites in a completely clean, grease-free mixing bowl. If any grease or even a speck of egg yolk is present, the egg whites will not hold air bubbles. Check and remove any specks of yolk.

2 Use a balloon whisk in a wide bowl for the greatest volume, though an electric hand whisk will also do an efficient job. Whisk the whites until they are firm enough to hold either soft or stiff peaks when you lift the whisk.

PREPARING NUTS

Nuts of all kinds make wonderful toppings and ingredients for ice creams. Some nuts may be bought complete with their brown, papery skins. The skin often has a bitter taste and so should be removed before the nuts are used. The flavour of all nuts is improved by toasting; this makes them appealingly crisp too.

1 To skin almonds and pistachios: put the nuts in a bowl and cover with boiling water. Leave for 2 minutes. (This is known as blanching.) Drain the nuts and cool slightly, then squeeze or rub each nut with your fingers to remove the skins.

2 To skin hazelnuts and brazils: spread the nuts on a baking sheet. Roast in a 180°C/350°F/Gas 4 oven for 10–15 minutes to dry the skins. Wrap the nuts in a clean dish towel and rub roughly to remove the skin.

3 To oven-roast or grill (broil) nuts: spread the nuts on a baking sheet. Roast in a 180°C/350°F/Gas 4 oven or under a moderate grill (broiler), until golden brown and smelling nutty. Stir the nuts occasionally to brown.

4 To dry-roast nuts: put the nuts in a frying pan, with no fat. Roast over moderate heat until golden brown. Stir constantly and watch carefully: nuts can scorch easily.

COOK'S TIP: It is very easy to burn nuts when dry-roasting. Nuts need only a few minutes so keep a careful eye on them.

5 To grind nuts: using a nut mill or a clean coffee grinder, grind a small batch of nuts at a time so that you can be sure of getting an even texture. As soon as the nuts have a fine texture, stop grinding: if overworked, they will turn to a paste.

6 You can also grind nuts in a food processor, but it is not as easy to get an even texture, and thus there is more risk of overworking the nuts to a paste. To prevent this, grind the nuts with some of the sugar or flour called for in the recipe.

MAKING CHOCOLATE CURLS
This method produces large chocolate curls which make an elegant decoration for ice creams.

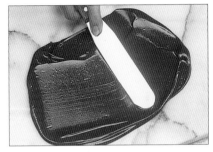

1 Melt plain (semisweet) or milk chocolate in a bowl set over barely simmering water. Spread the melted chocolate thinly and evenly over a marble slab or a cool, smooth work surface. Leave until it is just set.

2 Push a metal scraper or cheese slicer across the surface, at a 25° angle, to remove thin shavings of chocolate which should curl gently against the blade. If the chocolate sets too hard, it may become too brittle to curl and must be gently melted again.

Fresh Strawberry Ice Cream

You can make this ice cream by hand if you freeze it over a period of several hours, whisking it every hour or so.

Serves 6

INGREDIENTS
300 ml/½ pint/1¼ cups creamy milk
1 vanilla pod
3 large egg yolks
225 g/8 oz/2 cups strawberries
juice of ½ lemon
75 g/3 oz/¾ cup icing (confectioners') sugar
300 ml/½ pint/1¼ cups double (heavy) cream
sliced strawberries, to serve

1 Put the milk and the vanilla pod into a pan and bring to the boil over a low heat. Remove from the heat. Leave for 20 minutes, then remove the vanilla pod. Strain the milk into a bowl containing the egg yolks and whisk well.

2 Return the mixture to the clean pan and heat, stirring, until the custard just coats the back of the spoon. Pour the custard into a bowl, cover the surface with clear film (plastic wrap) and set aside to cool.

3 Meanwhile, purée the strawberries with the lemon juice in a food processor or blender. Press the strawberry purée through a sieve (strainer) into a bowl, then stir in the icing sugar and set aside.

4 Whip the cream to soft peaks, then gently but thoroughly fold it into the custard with the strawberry purée. Pour the mixture into an ice cream maker. Churn for 20–30 minutes, or until the mixture holds its shape.

5 Transfer the ice cream to a freezer container, cover and freeze until firm. Soften in the refrigerator for about 30 minutes before serving with the sliced strawberries.

COOK'S TIP: Use free-range eggs if possible, from a reputable supplier.

Mango Ice Cream with Exotic Fruit Salad

Exotic fruits are now widely available: choose your fruits with care, taking colour, shape and taste into account, then use them to create your own still life with this marvellous mango ice cream.

Serves 6–8

INGREDIENTS

2 large ripe mangoes, peeled, stoned (pitted)
    and roughly chopped
2 pieces preserved stem ginger
    plus 30 ml/2 tbsp ginger syrup
250 ml/8 fl oz/1 cup double (heavy) cream

FOR THE DECORATION

1 star fruit, thickly sliced
1 mango, peeled and cut into wedges
1 cantaloupe melon, cut into wedges
6 strawberries, cut in half
1 small bunch frosted grapes

1 Purée the mangoes in a food processor with the preserved ginger and ginger syrup, until smooth.

2 Whip the cream in a large bowl until it forms fairly firm peaks. Fold in the mango purée.

3 Transfer to a freezer container. Freeze for 2 hours, then beat with an electric mixer until smooth. Return the ice cream to the freezer and freeze for at least 8 hours. Alternatively, freeze in an ice cream maker according to the manufacturer's instructions.

4 About 30 minutes before serving, transfer the ice cream to the refrigerator to soften slightly. Arrange the prepared fruit on individual plates and add two scoops of ice cream to each one.

Avocado & Lime Ice Cream

In some parts of the world, avocados are frequently eaten as desserts. In fact, their rich texture makes them perfect for a smooth, creamy and delicious ice cream. The lime adds a touch of freshness to this dessert.

Serves 4–6

INGREDIENTS
4 egg yolks
300 ml/½ pint/1¼ cups whipping cream
115 g/4 oz/generous ½ cup sugar
2 ripe avocados, peeled and stoned (pitted)
grated rind of 2 limes
juice of 1 lime
2 egg whites
avocado slices and fresh mint, to decorate

1 Beat the egg yolks in a heatproof bowl. In a pan, heat the whipping cream with the sugar, stirring it well until it dissolves.

2 As the cream rises to the top of the pan at the point of boiling, remove it from the heat.

3 Gently pour the beaten egg yolks into the scalded cream, adding them in small amounts from a height above the pan. This stops the mixture from curdling. Allow the mixture to cool, stirring it occasionally, then chill.

4 Mash the avocados until they are smooth, then beat them into the custard with the lime rind and juice. Taste for sweetness; ice cream should be quite sweet before freezing as it loses flavour when ice-cold.

5 Pour the ice cream mixture into a shallow freezer container and freeze it until it is slushy. Remove from the freezer and beat it well to stop large ice crystals from forming. Return the mixture to the freezer for 3 hours and repeat the beating process once more.

6 Whisk the egg whites until softly stiff and fold into the ice cream. Return the mixture to the freezer and freeze until firm. Soften in the refrigerator for about 30 minutes before serving, decorated with avocado slices and sprigs of fresh mint.

COOK'S TIP: You can use an ice cream maker for this recipe but omit the egg whites as the paddle will beat in air.

Apricot Ice Cream under a Caramel Cage

Caramel is a favourite with confectioners because of its decorative possibilities. It is used here to create a delicate cage to cover a tea-scented apricot ice cream. It is sure to impress dinner party guests.

Serves 6–8

INGREDIENTS
450 g/1 lb/2 cups dried apricots
900 ml/1½ pints/3¾ cups cold
    Earl Grey tea
115 g/4 oz/½ cup soft light brown sugar
30 ml/2 tbsp brandy or gin
    (optional)
300 ml/½ pint/1¼ cups whipping cream

FOR THE DECORATION
500 g/1¼ lb/2½ cups
    caster (superfine) sugar
175 ml/6 fl oz/¾ cup water
120 ml/4 fl oz/½ cup liquid glucose (clear
    corn syrup)
oil, for greasing

1 Place the apricots in a large bowl. Pour the cold Earl Grey tea over, cover and soak the apricots for 4 hours or overnight.

2 Tip the apricots and the tea into a pan. Add the brown sugar. Bring to the boil, stirring to dissolve the sugar. Simmer gently for 15–20 minutes, until the apricots are tender. Allow to cool.

3 Process the apricots with the cooking liquid in a food processor to a rough purée; the apricots should be chopped but still identifiable. Stir in the brandy or gin, if using.

4 Whip the cream in a large bowl until soft peaks form. Fold in the apricot purée and mix well. Transfer to a freezer container and freeze for 2 hours. Beat with an electric mixer until smooth, then return to the freezer for at least 8 hours. Alternatively, place in an ice cream maker and freeze according to the manufacturer's instructions.

5 Meanwhile, make the decoration. Place the sugar and water in a small pan. Heat gently, stirring until the sugar dissolves. Bring to the boil and add the liquid glucose. Cook until the mixture is a pale caramel. Cool slightly. Lightly oil the back of a ladle.

6 Using a teaspoon, trail caramel over the upturned ladle in horizontal and vertical lines, until a "cage" is built. Leave to harden, then gently ease off. Repeat to make six to eight "cages". To serve, place a "cage" over scoops of ice cream.

Stem Ginger Ice Cream

This rich and flavourful ice cream goes beautifully with sliced fresh pears and bananas or with gooseberry and apple purée.

Serves 4

INGREDIENTS
15 ml/1 tbsp clear honey
4 egg yolks
600 ml/1 pint/2½ cups double (heavy) cream,
    lightly whipped
4 pieces preserved stem ginger, chopped into
    tiny dice

1 Place the honey and 150 ml/¼ pint/⅔ cup water in a small pan and heat until the honey is completely dissolved. Remove from the heat and allow to cool.

2 Place the egg yolks in a large bowl and whisk gently until pale and frothy. Slowly add the honey syrup and fold in the whipped cream.

3 Pour the mixture into a plastic freezer container and freeze for about 45 minutes, or until the ice cream is freezing at the edges.

4 Transfer to a bowl and whisk again. Mix in the stem ginger, reserving a few pieces for decoration. Freeze again for 2–4 hours. Serve in scoops, decorated with stem ginger.

Mint Ice Cream

For a special occasion, this fresh-tasting ice cream looks spectacular
served in an ice bowl which is made by freezing flower petals in water.

Serves 4–6

INGREDIENTS
8 egg yolks
75 g/3 oz/6 tbsp caster (superfine) sugar
600 ml/1 pint/2½ cups single (light) cream
1 vanilla pod
60 ml/4 tbsp chopped fresh mint
fresh mint sprigs, to decorate

1 Using an electric beater or balloon
whisk, beat the egg yolks and sugar
until pale and light. Transfer to a small
pan. In a separate pan, bring the cream
and vanilla pod to the boil.

2 Remove the pod and pour the hot
cream on to the egg mixture,
whisking. Continue whisking to
ensure that the eggs are mixed into the
cream. Gently heat the mixture until
the custard thickens enough to coat
the back of a wooden spoon. Cool.

3 Stir in the chopped mint, transfer
to a freezer container and freeze
until mushy. Whisk to break down
the ice crystals. Freeze for 3 hours,
then whisk again. Freeze for at least
6 hours, until hard. Serve, decorated
with mint sprigs.

Old-fashioned Chocolate Ice Cream

A classic and a great favourite with young and old alike.

Serves 8

INGREDIENTS
750 ml/1¼ pints/3 cups whipping cream
250 ml/8 fl oz/1 cup milk
1 vanilla pod, split in half
150 g/5 oz/¾ cup plus 2.5 ml/½ tsp caster
   (superfine) sugar
115 g/4 oz plain (semisweet) chocolate,
   grated
4 egg yolks

1 Put 250 ml/8 fl oz/1 cup of the whipping cream in a pan with the milk and the vanilla pod. Heat until bubbles appear at the edge of the pan.

2 Add 150 g/5 oz/¾ cup of the sugar and the chocolate. Heat almost to boiling point, stirring until the chocolate is melted and smooth.

3 In a bowl, lightly beat the egg yolks. Add the hot mixture, stirring constantly.

4 Pour into the top of a double pan set over hot water. Stir until the custard thickens enough to coat the spoon. Strain into a bowl. Stir in the remaining cream and sugar. Cool and then transfer to an ice cream maker and freeze. Serve in scoops.

Rippled Chocolate Ice Cream

A heavenly ice cream marbled with rich chocolate.

Serves 4

INGREDIENTS

60 ml/4 tbsp chocolate and hazelnut spread
450 ml/¾ pint/scant 2 cups double (heavy) cream
15 ml/1 tbsp icing (confectioners') sugar, sifted
50 g/2 oz plain (semisweet) chocolate
plain chocolate curls, to decorate

1 Mix together the chocolate and hazelnut spread and 75 ml/5 tbsp of the cream in a bowl. Place the remaining cream and the icing sugar in a second bowl and beat until whipped.

2 Chop the plain chocolate into small pieces.

3 Lightly fold in the chocolate mixture with the chopped chocolate until the mixture is rippled. Transfer to a freezer container and freeze for about 3–4 hours, until firm.

4 Remove the ice cream from the freezer about 30 minutes before serving to allow it to soften slightly. Spoon or scoop into dessert dishes or glasses and top each serving with a few plain chocolate curls.

White Chocolate Raspberry Ripple Ice Cream

Freeze ice cream in a soufflé dish or other attractive serving bowl so that it can be served directly at the table.

Serves 8

INGREDIENTS
250 ml/8 fl oz/1 cup milk
450 ml/¾ pint/scant 2 cups
   whipping cream
7 egg yolks
25 g/1 oz/2 tbsp sugar
225 g/8 oz fine-quality white
   chocolate, chopped
5 ml/1 tsp vanilla extract
fresh mint sprigs, to decorate

FOR THE RASPBERRY RIPPLE SAUCE
275 g/10 oz packet frozen
   raspberries in light syrup, thawed,
   or 275 g/10 oz jar reduced-sugar
   raspberry preserve
10 ml/2 tsp corn syrup
15 ml/1 tbsp lemon juice
15 ml/1 tbsp cornflour (cornstarch) mixed
   with 15 ml/1 tbsp water

1 To make the sauce, press the raspberries and their syrup through a sieve into a pan. Add the corn syrup, lemon juice and cornflour mixture. (If using raspberry preserve, omit the cornflour, but add the water.) Bring to the boil, stirring frequently, and simmer for 1–2 minutes, until syrupy. Pour into a bowl and cool, then refrigerate.

2 In a pan, bring the milk and 250 ml/8 fl oz/1 cup of the cream to the boil. Beat the egg yolks and sugar for 2–3 minutes with a hand-held mixer, until thick and creamy.

3 Pour the hot milk over the yolks and return to the pan. Cook gently until the custard coats the back of a wooden spoon, stirring constantly. Do not allow to boil or the custard will curdle.

4 Remove the pan from the heat and stir in the white chocolate until smooth. Pour the remaining cream into a medium bowl. Strain the hot custard into the bowl and add the vanilla. Blend and allow to cool to room temperature, then place in the refrigerater until cold. Transfer the custard to an ice cream maker and freeze according to the manufacturer's instructions.

5 When the mixture is frozen, but still soft, transfer one-third of the ice cream to a serving bowl. Spoon over some raspberry sauce. Cover with another third of the ice cream and more sauce. Cover with the remaining ice cream and more sauce.

6 With a knife or spoon, lightly marble the sauce into the ice cream. Cover and freeze until hard. Allow the ice cream to soften for about 30 minutes in the refrigerator before serving with the remaining raspberry sauce, decorated with mint.

Pistachio Halva Ice Cream

Halva is a sweet confection made from sesame seeds and is available in several flavours. This ice cream, studded with chunks of pistachio-flavoured halva, is as unusual as it is irresistible.

Serves 6

INGREDIENTS
3 egg yolks
115 g/4 oz/generous ½ cup caster (superfine) sugar
300 ml/½ pint/1¼ cups single (light) cream
300 ml/½ pint/1¼ cups double (heavy) cream
115 g/4 oz pistachio halva
chopped, unsalted pistachio nuts, to decorate

1 Whisk the egg yolks with the sugar in a bowl until thick and pale. Pour the single cream into a small pan and bring to the boil. Stir the hot cream into the egg-yolk mixture.

2 Transfer the mixture to a double boiler or a heatproof bowl placed over a pan of gently simmering water. Cook, stirring continuously, until the custard is thick enough to coat the back of a spoon. Strain into a bowl and leave to cool.

3 Whisk the double cream lightly, then whisk in the cooled custard. Crumble the halva into the mixture and stir in gently with a metal spoon.

4 Pour the halva mixture into a freezer container. Cover and freeze for 3 hours or until half-set. Stir well, breaking up any ice crystals, then return to the freezer until frozen solid. Alternatively, freeze in an ice cream maker, following the manufacturer's instructions.

5 Remove the ice cream from the freezer about 30 minutes before serving so that it softens enough for scooping. Serve decorated with chopped pistachio nuts.

COOK'S TIP: Other popular types of halva include pumpkin seed, sunflower seed, lentils, squash, carrots and yam.

Brown Bread & Hazelnut Ice Cream

Toasted breadcrumbs add to the sweet nuttiness of this ice cream, which is served with a tangy blackcurrant sauce.

Serves 6

INGREDIENTS
50 g/2 oz/½ cup roasted and chopped
    hazelnuts, ground
75 g/3 oz/1½ cups wholemeal breadcrumbs
50 g/2 oz/4 tbsp demerara (raw) sugar
3 egg whites
115 g/4 oz/generous ½ cup caster (superfine)
    sugar
300 ml/½ pint/1¼ cups double (heavy) cream
few drops of vanilla extract

FOR THE SAUCE
225 g/8 oz/2 cups blackcurrants
75 g/3 oz/6 tbsp caster (superfine) sugar
15 ml/1 tbsp crème de cassis
fresh mint sprigs, to decorate

1 Combine the hazelnuts and
breadcrumbs on a baking sheet,
then sprinkle over the demerara sugar.
Place under a medium grill (broiler)
and cook, stirring frequently, until the
mixture is evenly browned. Cool.

2 Whisk the egg whites in a bowl
until stiff, then gradually whisk in
the caster sugar until thick. Whip the
cream until it forms soft peaks and
fold into the meringue with the
breadcrumb and hazelnut mixture and
vanilla essence.

3 Spoon the mixture into a 1.2 litre/
2 pint/5 cup loaf tin (pan). Smooth
the top level, then cover and freeze for
several hours, or until firm.

4 Meanwhile, make the sauce. Strip
the blackcurrants from their stalks
and put the blackcurrants in a small
bowl with the caster sugar. Toss gently
to mix and leave for 30 minutes.

VARIATION: Replace the
hazelnuts with chopped almonds, if
you like.

5 Purée the blackcurrants in a blender or food processor, then press through a nylon sieve (strainer) until smooth. Add the crème de cassis and chill well.

6 To serve, turn out the ice cream on to a plate and cut into slices. Arrange each slice on a serving plate, spoon over a little sauce and decorate with fresh mint sprigs.

Hazelnut Ice Cream

This popular flavour is an especially good partner to chocolate ice cream.

Serves 4–6

INGREDIENTS
75 g/3 oz/¾ cup hazelnuts
30ml/2 tbsp sugar
475 ml/16 fl oz/2 cups milk
10 cm/4 in piece vanilla pod (bean)
4 egg yolks
75 g/3 oz/6 tbsp sugar

1 Spread the hazelnuts out on a baking sheet and place under a medium grill (broiler) for 5 minutes, shaking the pan to turn the nuts over. Remove from the heat and allow to cool slightly. Place the nuts on a dish towel and rub them with the cloth to remove their dark outer skin. Chop very finely, or grind in a food processor with 30 ml/2 tbsp sugar.

2 Make the custard. Heat the milk with the vanilla pod in a small pan. Remove from the heat as soon as small bubbles start to form on the surface. Do not let it boil.

3 Beat the egg yolks with a wire whisk or electric beater. Gradually incorporate the sugar and continue beating for about 5 minutes, until the mixture is pale yellow. Add the milk very gradually, pouring it in through a sieve and discarding the vanilla pod. Stir constantly until all the milk has been added.

4 Pour the mixture into the top of a double boiler, or into a heatproof bowl placed over a pan of simmering water. Add the chopped nuts. Stir over a moderate heat until the water in the pan is boiling and the custard thickens enough to lightly coat the back of a spoon. Remove from the heat and allow to cool.

5 Freeze in an ice cream maker following the manufacturer's instructions, or pour the mixture into a freezer container and freeze for about 3 hours until set. Remove from the container and chop roughly into 7.5 cm/3 in pieces. Place in the bowl of a food processor and process.

6 Return to the freezer container and freeze until firm. Repeat the freezing-chopping process two or three times, until a smooth consistency is achieved. Serve in scoops.

Pistachio & Almond Ice Cream

This unusual ice cream, based on an old Indian recipe, uses canned evaporated milk and is packed with nuts and dried and candied fruit.

Serves 4–6

INGREDIENTS
3 x 400 ml/14 fl oz cans evaporated milk
3 egg whites, whisked until peaks form
350 g/12 oz/3 cups icing (confectioners') sugar
5 ml/1 tsp ground cardamom
15 ml/1 tbsp rose water
175 g/6 oz/1½ cups pistachio nuts, chopped
75 g/3 oz/scant ½ cup sultanas (golden raisins)
75 g/3 oz/¾ cup flaked (sliced) almonds
25 g/1 oz glacé (candied) cherries, halved

2 Open the cans and empty the milk into a large, chilled bowl. Whisk until it doubles in quantity, then fold in the egg whites and icing sugar.

3 Gently fold in the remaining ingredients, seal the bowl with clear film and leave in the freezer for 1 hour.

1 Remove the labels from the cans of evaporated milk and lay the cans down in a pan with a tight-fitting cover. Fill the pan with water to reach three-quarters of the way up the cans. Bring to the boil, cover and simmer for 20 minutes. Leave to cool completely, then chill the cans in the refrigerator for 24 hours.

4 Remove from the freezer and mix using a fork. Transfer to a serving bowl and freeze again. Remove from the freezer 10 minutes before serving.

French-style Coupe Glacé with Chocolate Ice Cream

Extra-rich chocolate ice cream creates this luxurious dessert.

Serves 6

INGREDIENTS
225 g/8 oz dark (bittersweet) chocolate,
    chopped
250 ml/8 fl oz/1 cup milk mixed with
    250 ml/8 fl oz/1 cup single (light) cream
3 egg yolks
50 g/2 oz/generous ¼ cup sugar
350 ml/12 fl oz/1½ cups double (heavy)
    cream
15 ml/1 tbsp vanilla extract
chocolate triangles, to decorate

FOR THE ESPRESSO CREAM
45ml/3 tbsp instant espresso powder,
    dissolved in 45 ml/3 tbsp boiling water,
    cooled
350 ml/12 fl oz/1½ cups double (heavy)
    cream
30 ml/2 tbsp coffee-flavour liqueur

FOR THE CHOCOLATE ESPRESSO SAUCE
300 ml/½ pint/1¼ cups double (heavy) cream
30 ml/2 tbsp instant espresso powder,
    dissolved in 45 ml/3 tbsp boiling water
300 g/11 oz dark (bittersweet) chocolate,
    chopped
30 ml/2 tbsp coffee-flavour liqueur

1 Prepare the ice cream. In a pan over a low heat, melt the chocolate with 120 ml/4 fl oz/½ cup of the milk mixture, stirring frequently. Remove from the heat. In another pan, over medium heat, bring the remaining milk mixture gently to the boil.

2 In a bowl beat the egg yolks and sugar for 2–3 minutes with a hand-held mixer, until thick. Pour the hot milk mixture over the yolks, whisking constantly. Return to the pan and cook over medium heat until the custard thickens. (Do not boil or the custard will curdle.) Stir in the melted chocolate.

3 Pour the double cream into a bowl and strain the custard into the bowl. Add the vanilla. Cool, then refrigerate until cold. Transfer to an ice cream maker and freeze.

4 To make the espresso cream, stir the dissolved espresso powder into the cream and beat until soft peaks form. Add the liqueur and beat for 30 seconds. Spoon into an icing bag with a medium star nozzle and refrigerate.

5 Prepare the sauce. In a pan over medium heat, bring the cream and dissolved espresso powder to the boil. Remove from the heat and add the chocolate. Stir until melted. Add the liqueur and strain into a bowl. Keep warm.

6 To serve, soften the ice cream for 15 minutes at room temperature. Pipe a layer of espresso cream into the bottom of six wine goblets. Add scoops of ice cream. Spoon over the chocolate sauce and top with cream. Serve the remaining sauce separately.

33

Chocolate Mint Ice Cream Pie

Much simpler to make than you would expect from its luxurious appearance, this makes an excellent dessert for entertaining.

Serves 8

INGREDIENTS

75 g/3 oz/½ cup plain (semisweet) chocolate chips
40 g/1½ oz/3 tbsp butter or margarine
50 g/2 oz crisped rice cereal
1 litre/1¾ pints/4 cups mint-chocolate-chip ice cream
75 g/3 oz plain (semisweet) chocolate, to decorate

1 Line a 23 cm/9 in pie tin (pan) with foil. Place a round of baking parchment over the foil in the bottom of the tin.

2 In a heatproof bowl set over a pan of barely simmering water, or in a double boiler, melt the chocolate chips and butter or margarine. Remove the bowl from the heat and gently stir in the cereal, a little at a time. Leave to cool for 5 minutes.

3 Press the chocolate-cereal mixture evenly over the bottom and up the sides of the prepared tin (pan), forming a 1 cm/½ in rim. Refrigerate until hard.

4 Carefully remove the cereal base from the tin and peel off the foil and baking parchment. Return the base to the pie tin.

5 Remove the ice cream from the freezer and allow to soften for 10 minutes. Spread evenly in the crust. Freeze for about 1 hour, until firm.

6 For the decoration, have the chocolate at room temperature and draw the blade of a swivel-headed vegetable peeler along the smooth surface of the chocolate to shave off short, wide curls. Refrigerate the chocolate curls until needed and scatter them over the ice cream just before serving.

Coffee Ice Cream Sandwiches

A great combination of contrasting textures united by flavour: sweet, crunchy biscuits sandwiched together with cool, smooth ice cream.

Makes 8

INGREDIENTS
115 g/4 oz/½ cup butter or margarine,
   at room temperature
50 g/2 oz/generous ¼ cup caster (superfine)
   sugar
115 g/4 oz/1 cup plain (all-purpose) flour
30 ml/2 tbsp instant coffee powder
icing (confectioners') sugar, for dusting
450 ml/¾ pint/scant 2 cups coffee
   ice cream
30 ml/2 tbsp unsweetened cocoa powder

1 Lightly grease two or three large baking sheets.

2 With an electric mixer or wooden spoon, beat the butter or margarine until soft. Beat in the caster sugar. Add the flour and coffee and mix by hand to form an evenly blended dough. Wrap in a plastic bag and refrigerate for at least 1 hour.

3 Lightly dust a work surface with icing sugar. Knead the dough on the sugared surface for a few minutes to soften it slightly. Using a rolling pin dusted with icing sugar, roll out the dough to 3 mm/⅛ in thickness. With a 6 cm/2½ in fluted pastry cutter, cut out 16 rounds. Transfer the rounds to the prepared baking trays. Refrigerate for at least 30 minutes.

4 Preheat the oven to 150°C/300°F/ Gas 2. Bake the biscuits for about 30 minutes, until they are lightly golden. Leave the biscuits to cool and firm up before transferring them from the baking sheets to a wire rack to cool completely.

5 Remove the ice cream from the freezer and allow to soften for 10 minutes at room temperature. Spread the ice cream evenly over the flat side of eight of the biscuits and top with the remaining biscuits.

6 Arrange the ice cream sandwiches on a baking sheet. Cover and freeze for at least 1 hour, or longer if a firmer sandwich is desired. Sift the cocoa powder over the top before serving.

VARIATION: Other ice creams could be used for the filling as a contrast to the coffee biscuits. Try strawberry, vanilla or one containing chopped hazelnuts or almonds.

Amaretto Ice Cream in Brandy Snap Baskets

Amaretto, the almond-flavoured liqueur gives this ice cream a wonderful depth of flavour that is impossible to resist.

Serves 4–6

INGREDIENTS
750 ml/1¼ pints/3 cups vanilla ice
    cream, softened
30 ml/2 tbsp Amaretto
15 ml/1 tbsp orange juice
1.5 ml/¼ tsp vanilla extract
thinly pared orange rind,
    to decorate

FOR THE BRANDY SNAP BASKETS
50 g/2 oz/ 4 tbsp butter
50 g/2 oz/generous ¼ cup caster (superfine)
    sugar
75 g/3 oz/¼ cup golden (light corn) syrup
5 ml/1 tsp ground ginger
grated rind and juice of
    1 lemon
50 g/2 oz/½ cup plain (all-purpose) flour

1 Preheat the oven to 180°C/350°F/
Gas 4. Lightly grease and line
three baking sheets with baking
parchment.

2 Beat the vanilla ice cream until soft
and creamy, then beat in the
Amaretto, orange juice and vanilla
essence. Return to the tub, or a similar
container, for freezing. Set the freezer
at its coldest temperature and freeze
the ice cream until firm.

3 To make the brandy snap baskets,
put the butter, sugar, golden syrup
and ground ginger into a saucepan.
Heat gently, stirring constantly, until
the butter has melted, then turn off
the heat and stir in the lemon rind and
juice, followed by the flour.

4 The mixture hardens quickly, so
bake only two biscuits at a time.
Put spoonfuls of the mixture on to the
baking sheets. Bake for 10–12 minutes,
until golden. Cool for a few seconds.

5 Lift each biscuit in turn with a
palette knife and drape over a small
orange or the outside of an upturned
cup. Leave to cool and harden, then
invert on to plates. Add scoops of
Amaretto ice cream, decorate with
orange rind and serve.

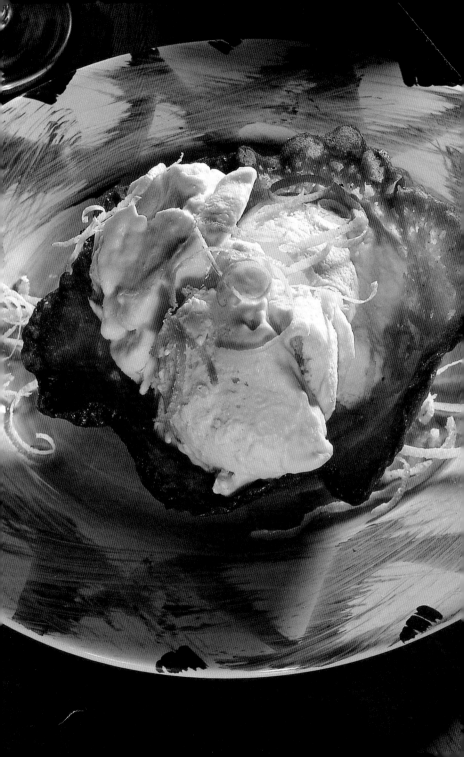

ffee & Chocolate Bombe

The delicious combination of Marsala and chocolate transforms bought ice cream in this sophisticated dessert.

Serves 6–8

INGREDIENTS
15–18 savoiardi (Italian sponge fingers)
about 175 ml/6 fl oz/¾ cup sweet Marsala
75 g/3 oz amaretti biscuits
about 475 ml/16 fl oz/2 cups coffee ice cream, softened
about 475 ml/16 fl oz/2 cups vanilla ice cream, softened
50 g/2 oz plain (bittersweet) chocolate, grated
chocolate curls and sifted cocoa powder or icing (confectioners') sugar, to decorate

1 Line a 1 litre/1¾ pint/4 cup pudding basin with a piece of damp muslin, letting it hang over the edge. Trim the sponge fingers to fit the basin.

2 Pour the Marsala into a dish. Quickly dip a sponge finger in the Marsala so that it becomes saturated but does not disintegrate. Stand it against the basin. Repeat with the other sponge fingers to line the basin.

3 Fill in the base and any gaps around the side with any trimmings and sponge fingers cut to fit. Chill for about 30 minutes.

4 Put the amaretti biscuits in a large bowl and crush them with a rolling pin. Add the coffee ice cream and any remaining Marsala and beat until mixed. Spoon into the sponge-finger-lined basin.

5 Press the ice cream against the sponge to form an even layer with a hollow in the centre. Freeze for 2 hours until firm.

6 Put the vanilla ice cream and grated chocolate in a bowl and beat together until evenly mixed. Spoon into the hollow in the centre of the mould. Smooth the top, then cover with the overhanging muslin. Place in the freezer overnight.

7 To serve, run a palette knife between the muslin and the basin, then unfold the top of the muslin. Invert a chilled serving plate on top, then invert the bowl so that the bombe is upside-down on the plate. Carefully peel off the muslin. Decorate the dessert with the chocolate curls, then sift cocoa powder or icing sugar over. Serve at once.

Blackcurrant Sorbet

This luscious sorbet is easily made by hand, but it is important to alternately freeze and blend or process the mixture five or six times.

Serves 6

INGREDIENTS
300 ml/½ pint/1¼ cups plus
   30 ml/2 tbsp water
115 g/4 oz/½ cup caster (superfine) sugar
225 g/8 oz/2 cups blackcurrants
30 ml/2 tbsp crème de cassis or other
   blackcurrant liqueur
5 ml/1 tsp lemon juice
2 egg whites

1 Pour 300 ml/½ pint/1¼ cups of the water into a pan and add the sugar. Place over a low heat until the sugar has dissolved. Bring to the boil and boil rapidly for 10 minutes, then set the syrup aside to cool.

2 Cook the blackcurrants with the remaining 30 ml/2 tbsp water over a low heat for 5–7 minutes. Press the blackcurrants and juice through a sieve (strainer), then stir the purée into the syrup with the liqueur and lemon juice. Cool, then chill for 1 hour.

3 Pour the chilled blackcurrant syrup into a freezerproof bowl and freeze until slushy, whisking occasionally. Whisk the egg whites in a grease-free bowl until soft peaks begin to form, then fold into the semi-frozen blackcurrant mixture.

4 Freeze the mixture again until firm, then spoon into a food processor and process or whisk by hand. Alternately freeze and process or whisk until completely smooth. Serve the sorbet straight from the freezer.

Raspberry Sorbet with a Soft Fruit Garland

A stunning fresh fruit and herb garnish creates a fabulous bold border for the scoops of deep red raspberry sorbet.

Serves 6–8

INGREDIENTS
175 g/6 oz/generous ¾ cup caster (superfine) sugar
250 ml/8 fl oz/1 cup water
450 g/1 lb/2⅔ cups fresh or thawed frozen raspberries
strained juice of 1 orange

FOR THE DECORATION
1 bunch fresh mint
selection of soft fruits, including strawberries, raspberries, redcurrants and blueberries

1 Heat the sugar with the water in a pan until dissolved, stirring occasionally. Bring to the boil, then set aside to cool. Purée the raspberries with the orange juice in a blender or food processor, then use a wooden spoon to press through a sieve to remove any seeds.

2 Mix the syrup with the puréed raspberries and pour into a freezer container. Freeze for 2 hours, or until ice crystals form around the edges of the sorbet. Whisk until smooth, then return to the freezer for 4 hours. Alternatively make the sorbet in an ice cream maker, according to the manufacturer's instructions.

3 About 30 minutes before serving, transfer the sorbet to the refrigerator to soften slightly. Place a large sprig of mint on the rim of a serving plate, then build up a garland, using more mint sprigs.

4 Leaving on the leaves, cut the strawberries in half. Arrange on the mint with the other fruit. Place the fruits at different angles and link the leaves with strings of redcurrants. Place scoops of sorbet in the centre and serve immediately.

Watermelon Sorbet

A slice of this refreshing and colourful sorbet is the perfect way to cool down on a hot, sunny day, and fun for children to eat too.

Serves 4–6

INGREDIENTS
½ small watermelon, weighing about
 1 kg/2¼ lb
75 g/3 oz/scant ½ cup caster (superfine)
 sugar
60 ml/4 tbsp cranberry juice or water
30 ml/2 tbsp lemon juice
fresh mint sprigs, to decorate

3 Put the caster sugar and cranberry juice or water in a medium heavy-based pan and stir over a low heat until the sugar dissolves. Bring to the boil and simmer for 5 minutes. Leave the sugar syrup to cool.

1 Cut the watermelon into 4–6 equal-size wedges (depending on the number of servings you require). Scoop out the pink flesh and set aside. Remove the seeds and discard. Reserve the shell.

2 Line a freezerproof bowl, about the same size as the melon, with clear film (plastic wrap). Arrange the melon skins in the bowl to re-form the shell, fitting them together snugly so that there are no gaps. Put in the freezer.

4 Put the melon flesh and lemon juice in a blender and process to a smooth purée. Stir in the sugar syrup and pour into a freezer container. Freeze for 3–3½ hours, or until slushy when tested with a fork.

5 Tip the sorbet into a chilled bowl and whisk to break up the ice crystals. Return to the freezer for another 30 minutes, whisk again, then tip into the melon shell and freeze until solid. To serve, cut through the individual slices of watermelon and sorbet and decorate with fresh mint.

Pink Grapefruit Sorbet

This tastebud-tingling citrus sorbet is the perfect way to clear the palate after a rich main course, and very easy to make.

Serves 8

INGREDIENTS
175 g/6 oz/generous ¾ cup sugar
120 ml/4 fl oz/½ cup water
1 litre/1¾ pints/4 cups strained
   freshly squeezed pink grapefruit juice
15–30 ml/1–2 tbsp lemon juice
icing (confectioners') sugar, to taste
fresh mint sprigs, to decorate

1 In a small, heavy pan, dissolve the sugar in the water over medium heat without stirring. When the sugar has dissolved, boil for 3–4 minutes. Remove from the heat and allow to cool.

2 Pour the cooled sugar syrup into the grapefruit juice. Stir well. Taste the mixture and adjust the flavour by adding some lemon juice or a little icing sugar, if necessary.

3 Pour the mixture into a freezer container and freeze for about 3 hours, until softly set.

4 Remove from the container and chop roughly into 7.5 cm/3 in pieces. Place in a food processor and process until smooth. Return the mixture to the freezer container and freeze again until set.

5 Repeat this freezing and chopping process two or three times, until a smooth consistency is obtained. Alternatively, freeze the sorbet in an ice cream maker, following the manufacturer's instructions. Serve in scoops, decorated with fresh mint.

VARIATION: For orange sorbet, substitute an equal amount of orange juice for the grapefruit juice and increase the lemon juice to 45–60 ml/3–4 tbsp or to taste.

Lime Sorbet

Use ripe, well-flavoured limes for this refreshing sorbet.

Serves 4

INGREDIENTS
250 g/9 oz/generous 1¼ cups
    sugar
600 ml/1 pint/2½ cups water
grated rind of 1 lime
175 ml/6 fl oz/¾ cup lime juice
15–30 ml/1–2 tbsp lemon juice
icing (confectioners') sugar, to taste
curls of lime rind, to decorate

1 In a small, heavy pan, dissolve the sugar in the water, without stirring, over medium heat. When the sugar has dissolved, boil for 5–6 minutes. Remove the syrup from the heat and set aside to cool.

2 Combine the cooled sugar syrup and lime rind and juice in a measuring jug or bowl. Stir the ingredients together thoroughly. Taste, and adjust the flavour by adding lemon juice or some icing sugar, if necessary. Be careful, however, not to over-sweeten.

3 Freeze the lime mixture in an ice cream maker, following the manufacturer's instructions. If you do not have an ice cream maker, pour the mixture into a freezer container and freeze for about 3 hours, until softly set.

4 Remove the mixture from the container and chop roughly into 7.5 cm/3 in pieces. Place in a food processor and process until smooth. Return the mixture to the freezer container and freeze again until set. Repeat this freezing and chopping process two or three times, until a smooth consistency is obtained.

COOK'S TIP: If using an ice cream maker for these sorbets, check the manufacturer's instructions to find out the freezing capacity. If necessary, halve the quantities used in the recipe. If too much mixture is placed in the bowl it will not set.

Chocolate Sorbet with Red Fruits

The chill that thrills – that's chocolate sorbet. For a really fine texture, it helps to have an ice-cream maker, which churns the mixture as it freezes, but you can make it by hand quite easily.

Serves 6

INGREDIENTS

475 ml/16 fl oz/2 cups water
45 ml/3 tbsp clear honey
115 g/4 oz/generous ½ cup caster (superfine) sugar
75 g/3 oz/¾ cup cocoa powder
50 g/2 oz plain (bittersweet) chocolate, broken into squares
400 g/14 oz soft red fruits, such as raspberries, redcurrants or strawberries

1 Place the water, honey, sugar and cocoa in a pan. Heat gently, stirring occasionally, until the sugar has completely dissolved.

2 Remove from the heat, add the chocolate and stir until melted. Leave until cool.

3 Tip into an ice cream maker and churn until frozen. Alternatively, pour into a freezer container, freeze until slushy, whisk until smooth, then freeze again. Whisk for a second time before the mixture hardens completely.

4 Remove from the freezer 10–15 minutes before serving so that the sorbet softens slightly. Serve in scoops, with the soft fruits.

COOK'S TIP: This sorbet looks attractive if served in small, oval scoops shaped with two spoons – simply scoop out the sorbet with one tablespoon, then use another to smooth it off and transfer it to the serving plate.

Iced Oranges

These little sorbets served in the fruit shell were originally sold in the beach cafés in the south of France. They are pretty and easy to eat – a good picnic treat to pack in the cool-box.

Serves 8

INGREDIENTS
150 g/5 oz/¾ cup sugar
juice of 1 lemon
120ml/4 fl oz/½ cup plus 90 ml/6 tbsp water
14 medium oranges
icing (confectioners') sugar, to taste
8 fresh bay leaves, to decorate

1 Put the sugar in a heavy-based pan. Add half the lemon juice and the water. Cook gently until the sugar has dissolved. Bring to the boil and boil for 2–3 minutes, until the syrup is clear. Leave to cool.

2 Slice the tops off 8 of the oranges, to make "hats" for the sorbets. Scoop out the flesh of the oranges and reserve. Put the empty orange shells and "hats" on a tray and place in the freezer until needed.

3 Grate the rind (zest) of the remaining oranges and add to the syrup. Squeeze the juice from the oranges and from the reserved flesh. There should be 750 ml/1¼ pints/3 cups. Squeeze another orange or add bought orange juice, if necessary.

4 Stir the orange juice, remaining lemon juice and 90 ml/6 tbsp water into the syrup. Taste, adding more lemon juice or icing sugar, as desired. Freeze the mixture in an ice cream maker, following the manufacturer's instructions. Alternatively, pour the mixture into a shallow freezer container and freeze for 3 hours.

5 Turn the mixture into a bowl and whisk to break down the ice crystals. Freeze for 4 hours more, until firm, but not solid.

6 Pack the mixture into the orange shells, mounding it up, and set the "hats" on top. Freeze until ready to serve. Just before serving, pierce the tops of the "hats" with a skewer and push a bay leaf into each hole.

COOK'S TIP: Use crumpled kitchen paper to keep the shells upright while the sorbet freezes.

Mango & Lime Sorbet in Lime Shells

This richly flavoured sorbet looks pretty served in the lime shells, but is also good served in scoops for a more traditional presentation.

Serves 4

INGREDIENTS
4 large limes
1 medium ripe mango
7.5 ml/1½ tsp powdered or leaf gelatine
2 egg whites
15 ml/1 tbsp caster (superfine) sugar
finely pared strips of lime rind, to decorate

3 Whisk the egg whites until they hold soft peaks. Whisk in the sugar. Fold the egg white mixture quickly into the mango mixture. Spoon the sorbet into the lime shells. Any leftover sorbet that will not fit into the lime shells can be frozen in small ramekins.

4 Overwrap the filled shells with clear film (plastic wrap), and place them in the freezer until the sorbet is firm. Before serving, remove the clear film and allow the shells to stand at room temperature for about 10 minutes; decorate them with strips of lime rind.

1 Cut a thick slice from the top of each of the limes, and then cut a thin slice from the bottom end so that the limes will stand upright. Squeeze the juice from the limes and reserve. Use a small knife to remove all the membrane from the centre.

2 Halve, stone, peel and chop the mango and purée the flesh in a food processor with 30 ml/2 tbsp of the lime juice. Dissolve the gelatine in 45ml/3 tbsp of the lime juice and stir it into the mango mixture.

COOK'S TIP: If you have lime juice left over from this recipe, it will freeze well for future use. Pour it into a small freezer container, seal it and freeze for up to six months.

Orange Granita with Strawberries

Granitas are like semi-frozen sorbets, but consist of larger particles of ice. Served in Italian cafés, they are very refreshing, particularly in the summer. For this jewel-like dessert use very juicy oranges and really ripe strawberries that do not need any additional sweetening.

Serves 4

INGREDIENTS
6 large juicy oranges
350 g/12 oz ripe strawberries
finely pared strips of orange rind,
    to decorate

1 Squeeze the juice from the oranges and pour into a shallow freezerproof bowl.

COOK'S TIP: Granita will keep for up to 3 weeks in the freezer. Sweet pink grapefruits or deep red blood oranges can be used for a different flavour and colour. Add a little freshly squeezed lemon juice if you prefer a more tart taste.

2 Place the bowl in the freezer set at its coldest temperature. Remove after 30 minutes and beat the semi-frozen juice thoroughly with a wooden spoon until it is smooth.

3 Repeat this beating and freezing process at 30-minute intervals over a 4-hour period. This will break the ice crystals down into small particles to give the correct consistency for an authentic granita.

4 Halve the fresh strawberries and arrange them on a serving plate. Scoop the granita into attractive serving glasses, decorate with strips of orange rind and serve immediately with the strawberries.

Summer Fruit Salad Ice Cream

What could be more cooling on a hot summer day than fresh summer fruits, lightly frozen in this irresistible ice?

Serves 6

INGREDIENTS
900 g/2 lb/6–7 cups mixed soft summer
    fruits, such as raspberries, strawberries,
    blackcurrants, redcurrants, etc.
2 eggs
225 g/8 oz/1 cup low fat Greek yogurt
175 ml/6 fl oz/¾ cup red grape juice
15 ml/1 tbsp powdered or leaf gelatine

1 Reserve half the fruit and purée the remainder in a food processor, or rub it through a sieve to make a smooth purée.

2 Separate the eggs and whisk the yolks and the yogurt into the mixed fruit purée.

3 Heat the grape juice until almost boiling, then remove it from the heat. Sprinkle the gelatine over the grape juice and stir to dissolve it.

4 Whisk the dissolved gelatine mixture into the fruit purée and then pour the mixture into a freezer container. Freeze until half-frozen and slushy in consistency.

5 Whisk the egg whites with an electric hand-held mixer until they are stiff. Quickly fold them into the half-frozen mixture.

6 Return to the freezer and freeze until almost firm. Scoop into individual serving dishes or glasses and add the reserved soft fruits.

COOK'S TIP: Red grape juice has a good flavour and improves the colour of the ice, but if it is not available, use cranberry, apple or orange juice instead.

Buttermilk Vanilla Ice Cream

Enriched with a little fresh cream, this unusual ice cream tastes far more luxurious than it really is. Serve it with fresh fruit or fruit purée.

Serves 4

INGREDIENTS
250 ml/8 fl oz/1 cup buttermilk
60 ml/4 tbsp double (heavy) cream
1 vanilla pod (bean) or 2.5 ml/½ tsp vanilla
    extract
2 eggs
30 ml/2 tbsp clear honey

1 Place the buttermilk and cream in a pan with the vanilla pod, if using, and heat gently until the mixture is almost boiling. Remove the vanilla pod.

2 Place the eggs in a heatproof bowl over a pan of hot water and whisk until they are pale and thick.

3 Pour in the heated buttermilk in a thin stream, whisking hard. Continue whisking over the hot water until the mixture thickens slightly and coats the back of a spoon.

4 Whisk in the clear honey and vanilla extract, if using. Spoon the mixture into a freezer container and freeze until firm.

5 When the mixture is firm enough to hold its shape, spoon it on to a sheet of non-stick baking paper. Form it into a long smooth sausage shape and roll it up in the paper. Freeze again until it is firm. Serve the ice cream in slices.

Cranberry Bombe

This attractive dessert features smooth buttermilk vanilla ice cream enclosing a colourful cranberry and orange sorbet.

Serves 6

INGREDIENTS
FOR THE SORBET CENTRE
175 g/6 oz/1½ cups fresh or frozen
  cranberries
150 ml/¼ pint/⅔ cup orange juice
finely grated rind of ½ orange
2.5 ml/½ tsp ground mixed (apple-pie) spice
50 g/2 oz/generous ¼ cup golden
  caster (superfine) sugar

FOR THE OUTER LAYER
1 quantity Buttermilk Vanilla Ice Cream
30 ml/2 tbsp chopped angelica
30 ml/2 tbsp chopped mixed peel
15 ml/1 tbsp flaked (sliced) almonds,
  toasted

1 For the sorbet, put the cranberries, orange juice, rind and spice in a pan and cook gently until the fruit is soft. Add the sugar, then purée until almost smooth. Leave to cool.

2 Allow the vanilla ice to soften slightly, then stir in the chopped angelica, mixed peel and almonds.

3 Pack into a 1.2 litre/2 pint/5 cup pudding basin and hollow out the centre. Freeze until firm.

4 Fill the hollowed-out centre of the bombe with the cranberry mixture, smooth over and freeze until firm. To serve, turn out and cut into slices.

Index

This edition is published by Lorenz Books, an imprint of Anness Publishing Ltd, Blaby Road, Wigston, Leicestershire LE18 4SE; info@anness.com

www.lorenzbooks.com; www.annesspublishing.com

If you like the images in this book and would like to investigate using them for publishing, promotions or advertising, please visit our website www.practicalpictures.com for more information.

© Anness Publishing Limited 2013

A CIP catalogue record for this book is available from the British Library.

Publisher: Joanna Lorenz
Editor: Valerie Ferguson & Helen Sudell
Series Designer: Bobbie Colgate Stone
Designer: Andrew Heath
Production Controller: Steve Lang

Recipes contributed by: Catherine Atkinson, Angela Boggiano, Janet Brinkworth, Carla Capalbo, Frances Cleary, Roz Denny, Rafi Fernandez, Christine France, Sarah Gates, Shirley Gill, Janine Hosegood, Gilly Love, Lesley Mackley, Norma MacMillan, Maggie Mayhew, Liz Trigg, Laura Washburn, Elizabeth Wolf-Cohen, Jeni Wright

Photography: William Adams-Lingwood, Karl Adamson, Edward Allwright, Steve Baxter, James Duncan, Michelle Garrett, Amanda Heywood, Janine Hosegood, David Jordan, Don Last, Michael Michaels, Thomas Odulate.

NOTES

Bracketed terms are intended for American readers. For all recipes, quantities are given in both metric and imperial measures and, where appropriate, in standard cups and spoons. Follow one set of measures, but not a mixture, because they are not interchangeable. Standard spoon and cup measures are level. 1 tsp = 5ml, 1 tbsp = 15ml, 1 cup = 250ml/8fl oz. Australian standard tablespoons are 20ml. Australian readers should use 3 tsp in place of 1 tbsp for measuring small quantities. American pints are 16fl oz/2 cups. American readers should use 20fl oz/2.5 cups in place of 1 pint when measuring liquids. Electric oven temperatures in this book are for conventional ovens. When using a fan oven, the temperature will probably need to be reduced by about 10–20°C/20–40°F. Since ovens vary, you should check with your manufacturer's instruction book for guidance. Medium (US large) eggs are used unless otherwise stated.

PUBLISHER'S NOTE